VanDerZee

A Book of Postcards

Pomegranate

SAN FRANCISCO

Pomegranate Communications, Inc.
Box 6099
Rohnert Park, CA 94927
www.pomegranate.com

Pomegranate Europe Ltd.
Fullbridge House, Fullbridge
Maldon, Essex CM9 4LE
England

ISBN 0-7649-0708-5
Pomegranate Catalog No. A521

Pomegranate publishes books of
postcards on a wide range of subjects.
Please write to the publisher for more information.

Designed by Shannon Lemme
Printed in Korea
07 06 05 04 03 02 01   10 9 8 7 6 5 4 3 2

To facilitate detachment of the postcards from this book, fold each card along its perforation line before tearing.

Photographer James VanDerZee (1886–1983) is best known as a chronicler of Harlem life of the 1920s and 1930s, and particularly of the ten-year-long artistic explosion known as the Harlem Renaissance, that began around 1919. His images, thirty outstanding examples of which appear in this book of postcards, offer an amazing insight into the values of black middle-class American life of that time and reveal much about the essential nature of Harlem. He undertook work for churches, businesses, the celebrities and leaders of Harlem, schools, and organizations such as the United Negro Improvement Association (UNIA), documenting activities often ignored in the general press.

The Metropolitan Museum of Art featured VanDerZee's photographs of Harlem in the multimedia exhibition "Harlem On My Mind." When the exhibition opened on January 18, 1969, the eighty-one-year-old photographer saw his work presented and appreciated as never before. Since that time, VanDerZee's work has been exhibited throughout this country and Europe.

Later in his life, VanDerZee created portraits of some of the country's most famous African American celebrities. His photographic body of work is a national treasure, both as art and as cultural history.

V A N D E R Z E E

James VanDerZee (American, 1886–1983)

My Corsage, 1931

Pomegranate

BOX 6099, ROHNERT PARK, CA 94927

V A N D E R Z E E

James VanDerZee (American, 1886–1983)

Sunday Drive, c. 1932

BOX 6099, ROHNERT PARK, CA 94927

Pomegranate

VanDerZee

James VanDerZee (American, 1886–1983)

Boys in Sailor Suits, 1935

Pomegranate · BOX 6099, ROHNERT PARK, CA 94927

VanDerZee

James VanDerZee (American, 1886–1983)

Bathing Beauty, 1926

BOX 6099, ROHNERT PARK, CA 94927

Pomegranate

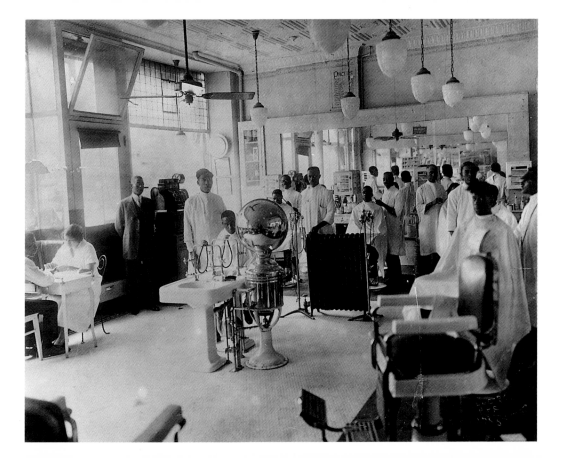

V A N D E R Z E E

James VanDerZee (American, 1886–1983)

Barbershop, 1925

Pomegranate

BOX 6099, ROHNERT PARK, CA 94927

VanDerZee

James VanDerZee (American, 1886–1983)

Evening Appearance, 1931

BOX 6099, ROHNERT PARK, CA 94927

Pomegranate

VanDerZee

James VanDerZee (American, 1886–1983)

Sunday Morning, New York City, c. 1925

Pomegranate

BOX 6099, ROHNERT PARK, CA 94927

VanDerZee

James VanDerZee (American, 1886–1983)

Alonzo, 1924

BOX 6099, ROHNERT PARK, CA 94927

Pomegranate

V A N D E R Z E E

James VanDerZee (American, 1886–1983)

Billie, 1926

Pomegranate

BOX 6099, ROHNERT PARK, CA 94927

V a n D e r Z e e

James VanDerZee (American, 1886–1983)

Father's Day, 1939

Pomegranate · BOX 6099, ROHNERT PARK, CA 94927

VanDerZee

James VanDerZee (American, 1886–1983)

At the Beach, date unknown

BOX 6099, ROHNERT PARK, CA 94927

Pomegranate

VanDerZee

James VanDerZee (American, 1886–1983)

The Secretary, 1929

BOX 6099, ROHNERT PARK, CA 94927

Pomegranate

V A N D E R Z E E

James VanDerZee (American, 1886–1983)

Souvenir from New York City, 1936

BOX 6099, ROHNERT PARK, CA 94927

Pomegranate

VanDerZee

James VanDerZee (American, 1886–1983)

Alpha Phi Alpha Basketball Team, 1926

BOX 6099, ROHNERT PARK, CA 94927

Pomegranate

VanDerZee

James VanDerZee (American, 1886–1983)

Gypsy Dancer, 1923

BOX 6099, ROHNERT PARK, CA 94927

Pomegranate

V A N D E R Z E E

James VanDerZee (American, 1886–1983)

The One I Love, 1937

BOX 6099, ROHNERT PARK, CA 94927

Pomegranate

V A N D E R Z E E

James VanDerZee (American, 1886–1983)

Whittier Preparatory School (#2), c. 1908

Pomegranate   BOX 6099, ROHNERT PARK, CA 94927

VanDerZee

James VanDerZee (American, 1886–1983)

Bridesmaids in Harlem, c. 1930

Pomegranate BOX 6099, ROHNERT PARK, CA 94927

VAN DER ZEE

James VanDerZee (American, 1886–1983)

Adorned in Pearls, 1924

BOX 6099, ROHNERT PARK, CA 94927

Pomegranate

VanDerZee

James VanDerZee (American, 1886–1983)

Friendship Is, c. 1908

BOX 6099, ROHNERT PARK, CA 94927

Pomegranate

VanDerZee

James VanDerZee (American, 1886–1983)

The Wedding Party, 1932

Pomegranate   BOX 6099, ROHNERT PARK, CA 94927

VanDerZee

James VanDerZee (American, 1886–1983)

A Boy's Best Friends, 1934

Pomegranate · BOX 6099, ROHNERT PARK, CA 94927

V A N D E R Z E E

James VanDerZee (American, 1886–1983)

The Blessing of Elders, 1926

Pomegranate BOX 6099, ROHNERT PARK, CA 94927

VANDERZEE

James VanDerZee (American, 1886–1983)

St. Marks School, 1928

Pomegranate   BOX 6099, ROHNERT PARK, CA 94927

VᴀɴDᴇʀZᴇᴇ

James VanDerZee (American, 1886–1983)

Couple in Raccoon Coats, 1932

BOX 6099, ROHNERT PARK, CA 94927

Pomegranate

VanDerZee

James VanDerZee (American, 1886–1983)

Kate and Rachel, c. 1908

Pomegranate   BOX 6099, ROHNERT PARK, CA 94927

VanDerZee

James VanDerZee (American, 1886–1983)

Atlantic City, c. 1925

BOX 6099, ROHNERT PARK, CA 94927

Pomegranate